PLAINS INDIANS

Kate Hayden

Hello, I'm
White Buffalo

Come and explore
MY WORLD and
find out what it's like
to be a Plains Indian.

I'm called
Eagle Dog

My name is
Chased-by-Bears

in association with
FRANKLIN WATTS

Created by
Two-Can Publishing Ltd
346 Old Street
London
EC1V 9NQ

Art direction and design: Helen McDonagh
Editor: Jacqueline McCann
Consultant: Colin Taylor (except pages 6 and 9)
Managing Editor: Christine Morley
Managing Art Director: Carole Orbell
Cover design: Helen Holmes
Model maker: Melanie Williams
Illustrator: David Hitch
Photography: John Englefield

Additional photography by Jon Barnes, and model design by Andrew Haslam on
p4-5 (c), p6 (l), p9, p10-11, p17 (br), p21 (r), p23 (tl), p24 (tr), p25 (cr).
Story and pictographs on page 27 adapted from 'Indian Talk', by Iron-Eyes Cody.

This edition published by Two-Can Publishing Ltd in 1997
in association with
Franklin Watts
96 Leonard Street
London
EC2A 4RH

Hardback ISBN 1 85434 459 5
Dewey Decimal Classification 970.004

Hardback 2 4 6 8 10 9 7 5 3 1

A catalogue record for this book is available from the British Library.

Printed in Hong Kong by Wing King Tong

CONTENTS

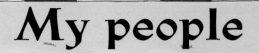

My name is White Buffalo and I'm eight years old. I was born in 1867 in a Sioux Indian camp here in the Great Plains of North America. The Plains is a vast area of grassland, home to many Indians.

American Indians live all over North America. We live in large groups called tribes. I belong to the Sioux tribe.

Plains Indians live on the land inside this red line. The Sioux tribe is only one of about 20 tribes that live here.

The Comanche and the Crow also live on the Plains. The Sioux trade with them sometimes, but we fight with them too.

The Tarahumara live south of the Plains, in Mexico. Many of them live in caves high in the mountains.

The Montagnais live and fish near this river. Their homes are made from the bark of trees.

The Iroquois live near these lakes. They build homes of wood and bark. They're good farmers and grow corn and pumpkins.

The Seminoles live in reed houses, built on the marshy land in Florida.

Signs on the map

where the buffalo roam

where Plains Indians live

forest areas

North-American Indians

Indians like me have been living in North America for thousands of years. Each tribe has its own language, customs and beliefs. Some tribes live in one place all the time, but Plains Indians spend most of the year on the move, following the huge herds of buffalo that roam the Plains. We couldn't survive here without the buffalo because our food comes from them. We use their hides to make our clothes and homes too.

White Buffalo

I'm proud of my name. The white buffalo is a rare animal, which makes it special. My grandmother was named after a white buffalo because she once saw one. Sometimes Indians name themselves after an important event, or maybe an unusual dream. We can change our names too if we like, when we're older.

5

My home is called a tipi. I share it with my mother, father and brother, Chased-by-Bears. During the day, while the men hunt buffalo, I help Mother tidy the tipi and collect firewood. When I've finished my chores, I play with my friends, or with my doll and her cradle.

When I was a baby, my mother carried me in a cradle like this, strapped to her back, or to a horse's saddle.

My cousin is collecting wood to build a fire outside the tipi.

Sioux girls

When I am about fifteen, Mother says I will be ready for marriage. That's when most of the girls in my village get married. I still have a lot to learn before then, such as how to make a tipi, and sew skins to make clothes and moccasins.

Sioux braves

Chased-by-Bears will be ten soon, so he'll be old enough to go hunting. My father is a skilful hunter and warrior, and he will teach my brother all he needs to know. By the time Chased-by-Bears is sixteen, he'll be a young warrior, or brave, ready to go to war.

Eagle Dog has painted himself like a Sioux warrior going to battle.

Chased-by-Bears is practising his fighting skills with his friend, Eagle Dog.

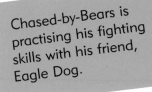

7

When we move to new hunting grounds we take everything with us, even our tipi. It's my job to help roll it up, along with all the bedding, and load it on to a horse. Then, at the new camp, I help unpack everything.

Building a home

Last year, Mother made a new tipi. First, she made a frame of wooden poles. Then she sewed six buffalo skins together for a cover. I helped to paint a pattern on the tipi, so that the people of our village will recognize our home.

Let's make a tipi ✳ Adult help needed

Find calico 4.5m x 2m, a circle of calico 0.5m in diameter, scissors, rope, acrylic paints, paintbrush, 14 canes 2.5m long, 15 sticks. Put your tipi up outside.

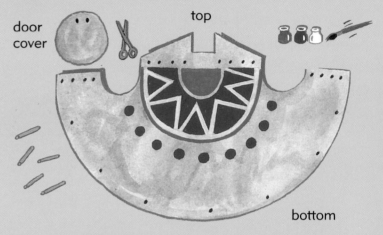

1 Cut out this tipi shape from the larger piece of fabric. Make 23 small holes where you see the dots. Paint a design on your tipi.

2 Using the rope, tie 3 canes together at one end to make a tripod. One by one, tie in the remaining canes at the top, to make a frame.

3 Wrap the fabric around the frame. Use 8 sticks to hold it in place (see the photo right). Hang the circle of fabric from the stick above the entrance.

4 Peg the tipi down with the other 7 sticks.

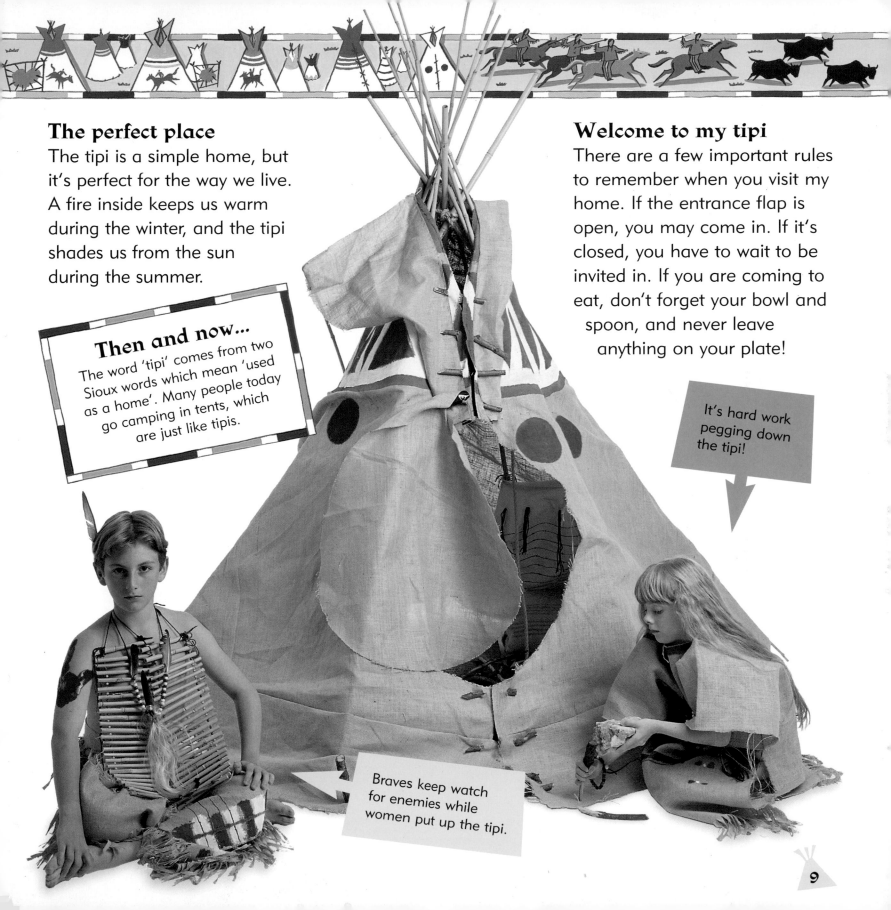

The perfect place

The tipi is a simple home, but it's perfect for the way we live. A fire inside keeps us warm during the winter, and the tipi shades us from the sun during the summer.

Then and now...

The word 'tipi' comes from two Sioux words which mean 'used as a home'. Many people today go camping in tents, which are just like tipis.

Welcome to my tipi

There are a few important rules to remember when you visit my home. If the entrance flap is open, you may come in. If it's closed, you have to wait to be invited in. If you are coming to eat, don't forget your bowl and spoon, and never leave anything on your plate!

It's hard work pegging down the tipi!

Braves keep watch for enemies while women put up the tipi.

9

Our tipi village

Altogether, there are 20 tipis in my village. Every summer we meet up with lots of other Sioux villages and travel around the Plains. We have a special hand signal for 'tipi' – just cross your fingers like this.

Choosing a camp

It's not always easy to find a good camp. We need fresh water for drinking and cooking, so the best place for a tipi is a sheltered spot by a river or stream. There's often a very strong wind that blows across the Plains, so Mother makes sure that the tipi entrance faces the opposite way.

These are some of the tipis from my village. We are camped by a river.

This wooden tipi frame will soon be covered with buffalo skins.

Buffalo skins are stretched and softened before they're made into tipi coverings.

In summer, we dry strips of buffalo meat in the sun to eat in winter.

Village life

There's always lots to do during the day. While the men are hunting, women prepare deer and buffalo skins for making tipis, bags, clothes and blankets. The skins have to be pegged out in the sun, scraped clean and softened before they can be used. It's hard work, and I have to help too.

The end of the day

In the evening, when the men return from hunting, we eat. If they've caught buffalo, we have fresh meat, but if not, we eat dried meat instead. Later on, my friends and I sit around the camp fire and listen to stories about our ancestors and the spirits.

Coloured streamers send messages to the spirits.

This flap lets out smoke from the fire inside the tipi.

Each family paints its tipi differently.

11

Long plaits are a sign of beauty for Sioux girls.

Our clothes are made from deerskin, which is really soft. Everyone wears leggings and moccasins – girls wear them with dresses, and boys wear them with shirts. We only wear our best clothes on special days.

Let's make a pair of moccasins

Find 0.5m of calico, felt pen, pins, scissors, needle, thread, cold tea, acrylic paints, paintbrush.

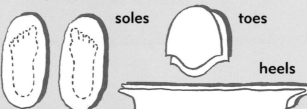

soles   toes

heels

1 Stand on the fabric and draw around your feet. Draw the heel and toe shapes on to the fabric (make the toe 2cm wider than the sole). Cut out 2 of each of the shapes.

2 Pin the heel around the edge of the sole. Then pin the toe piece on as shown in the picture below. Pin the edges where the heel and toe meet.

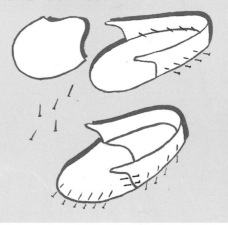

My best dress has fringes all around the edges.

Dresses and moccasins

My mother made my dress from two deerskins. She made my moccasins too. The tops are deerskin and the soles are buffalo hide, which is much tougher. For decoration, mother sewed on lots of tiny, bright beads, quills and feathers.

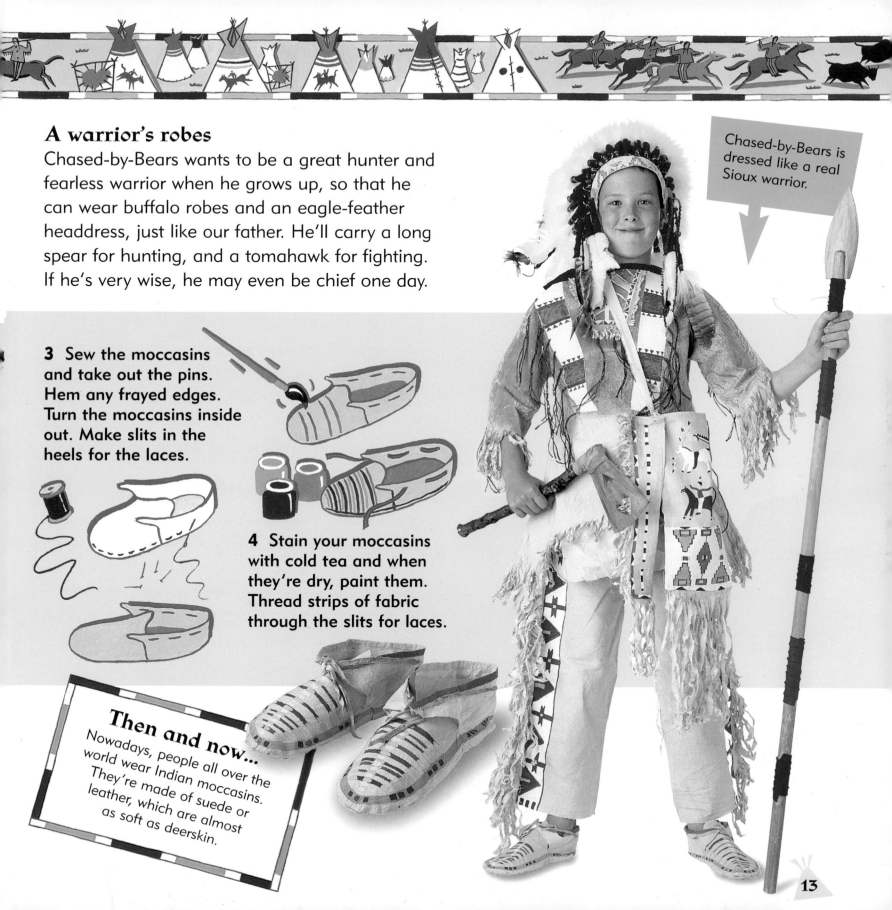

A warrior's robes

Chased-by-Bears wants to be a great hunter and fearless warrior when he grows up, so that he can wear buffalo robes and an eagle-feather headdress, just like our father. He'll carry a long spear for hunting, and a tomahawk for fighting. If he's very wise, he may even be chief one day.

Chased-by-Bears is dressed like a real Sioux warrior.

3 Sew the moccasins and take out the pins. Hem any frayed edges. Turn the moccasins inside out. Make slits in the heels for the laces.

4 Stain your moccasins with cold tea and when they're dry, paint them. Thread strips of fabric through the slits for laces.

Then and now...
Nowadays, people all over the world wear Indian moccasins. They're made of suede or leather, which are almost as soft as deerskin.

Beads and quills

The Sioux don't have many belongings. Everything we own has to be useful, but it can look beautiful at the same time. Men and women wear clothes decorated with bright beads and porcupine quills, and we make jewellery too.

Some warriors wear necklaces made from bear claws.

My necklace is made of shells which have come all the way from the sea.

A bear-claw necklace

Any man who wears bear claws must be very brave, because he has to fight a bear to get them. Warriors believe that wearing bear claws will make them fierce and strong, like bears.

Patterns with beads and quills

Sioux women spend hours sewing beads and weaving quills on to clothes. Quills are long spikes from the porcupine. Mother flattens the quills and dyes them. Then she weaves them in patterns that look like some of the things we see around us, such as a tipi, or a mountain.

We make these patterns with beads and quills.

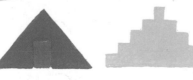

tipi   mountain   arrow   forked tree

Let's make a lucky hunting pouch

Find 0.5m of calico, pen, scissors, pins, cold tea, needle, thread, beads.

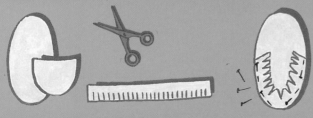

1 Draw the 3 shapes shown, above left, on the fabric. Cut them out. For a fringe, make lots of snips along one side of the long strip. Pin the fringe to the edge of the oval shape, so that the fringe points inwards.

2 Sew the half-oval shape to the fringe. Carefully turn the pouch inside out and remove the pins.

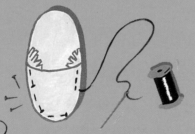

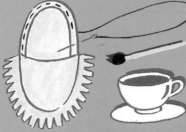

3 Hem the top flap of fabric. To make the pouch look like hide, stain it with cold tea then leave it to dry.

4 Draw a design on the pouch, then sew on the coloured beads to make a pattern. Sew on 4 or 5 beads at a time.

5 For a strap, sew a long strip of fabric on to the pouch.

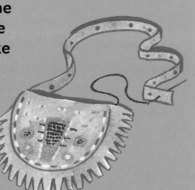

Lucky hunting pouch

My friend Eagle Dog has a beaded pouch that he wears when he goes hunting. He keeps small tools, such as arrowheads inside. The pattern on the pouch works like a lucky charm to ward off any danger when he hunts.

Eagle Dog keeps his hunting tools in his lucky pouch.

The food we eat

The Sioux are always moving from one hunting ground to another, so there's no time to plant and grow food. Instead, we hunt wild buffalo and deer for most of the year, and gather berries and vegetables in the summer. We trade too, for things that we cannot find ourselves.

Here are some of the things that Plains Indians like to eat.

 wild turnip sugar cane

 coffee berries nuts corn fish

buffalo moose deer pronghorn antelope

Sometimes we cook food in buffalo-hide pots.

Food on the Plains

My favourite meal of all is buffalo stew which Mother cooks in a pot over the fire. The meat and vegetables go in first, then water and, last of all, very hot stones. The stones make the water boil, which cooks the stew. When the stew is ready, we take out the stones and tuck in.

Trading with the white man

We have to trade for things we can't find on the Plains. When my mother was a girl, we didn't have coffee or sugar. Now we swap buffalo hides for them with the white man.

Meat for the winter

When Father returns from a hunt with a deer or buffalo, we only eat a little of the meat. We cut the rest up into strips and dry them in the sun. Dried meat is called 'jerky' and we keep it for winter, when fresh meat is hard to come by.

Sharing food

The Plains are bitterly cold in winter and deep snow makes it difficult to hunt buffalo or find food. So everyone in the village shares whatever food they have. If we have visitors to our tipi, Mother always makes sure they eat first.

Let's make corn cakes ★ Adult help needed

Find 3 or 4 corn-on-the-cob, half a cup of cornmeal flour, water, quarter cup of honey, saucepan, bowl, spoon, cup.

1 Peel off 14 leaves from the cobs. Ask an adult to boil the leaves until they're soft.

2 Put the cornmeal in a bowl. Ask an adult to slowly add a cup of boiling water to the cornmeal and stir until it is thick like custard. Add the honey.

3 Flatten the leaves and drop 2 spoonfuls of mixture into the middle of 10 of them. Fold the leaves into neat parcels and tie them with long shreds from the other 4 leaves.

4 Boil the parcels for about 15 to 20 minutes. Then drain them and leave them to cool. Now unwrap them and taste!

Trading with other Indians

We are often at war with other Indians over hunting grounds, but in peace time, we trade. We get corn and vegetables from the Crow who spend a lot of time in the north of the Plains. Grain and vegetables grow well there.

Corn cakes are delicious. The Hopi Indians were the first to make them.

Sioux men earn respect by showing courage and skill when they hunt and fight. Warriors put on war paint when they prepare for battle, to make themselves seem fierce. Women also wear war paint until the men return home safely from battle.

The buffalo hunt

It will take Chased-by-Bears a few years to be a successful hunter. It takes a lot of patience to hunt buffalo, so when a Sioux brave makes his first kill it's an important event. One way to hunt buffalo is to creep up on them quietly. My father sometimes wears a wolfskin when he's hunting, so that the buffalo can't see or smell him coming.

Chased-by-Bears has disguised himself as a wolf. He's practising stalking the buffalo.

A warrior never goes into battle without his war club.

A warrior's shield

When my father goes into battle against the Crow or the Comanche, he takes his war club and shield. His shield is very special to him. The eagle feathers and symbols on it help to protect my father from his enemies. We call this 'good medicine'.

Before a battle

Before a battle begins, the warriors burn a little of the sweetgrass that grows on the Plains. Then they sing special songs to the spirits so that the warriors will be protected on the battlefield.

Then and now...

Eagles are not only powerful symbols, or signs, for Indians. Today the eagle is also a national symbol for the USA.

Let's make an eagle shield

Find card, 0.5m of calico, scissors, glue, pencil, acrylic paints, paintbrush, 8 feathers, 4 strips of red felt, needle, thread, tape.

1 Cut a card circle 30cm in diameter. Now cut a slightly larger circle of fabric and glue it to the card as shown.

2 Draw an eagle design on to your shield. Now paint it. Let each colour dry before starting another one.

3 Wrap a strip of red felt around a pair of feathers. Sew them to the edge of the shield. Do the same with the other feathers.

4 For a handle, cut a thick strip of card and bend it gently to form a curve. Tape the ends firmly to the back of the shield.

My people believe that golden eagles are kings of the sky and of thunder, because they are swift and fly near the sun. Golden-eagle feathers are prized among Sioux warriors, who use them to make headdresses. You can tell how important a warrior is by looking at the feathers in his hair.

The golden-eagle feathers worn by Sioux braves show what happened to them in battle.

On special days, I wear a tail feather from a golden eagle in my hair.

| I've been wounded | I defeated my enemy | I've been wounded many times | I wounded my enemy |

Golden-eagle feathers

A Sioux brave earns the right to wear an eagle feather when he has shown great skill in battle. He marks the feather to show what happened to him. Each cut or spot of colour on a feather means something which other Sioux can understand.

The more feathers a warrior has, the more important he is. After many years and successful battles, some warriors, like my father, win enough feathers to make a full Sioux headdress. It's called a war-bonnet.

The war-bonnet

A warrior must have the approval of the other men of the village before he can wear a war-bonnet. Then, he may wear it into battle and to the Sun-dance. We believe that even wearing one eagle feather brings good medicine, so there must be a lot in a war-bonnet.

Buffalo-horn headdress

I think my father hopes that one day he'll be chief and wear a buffalo-horn headdress. Only the wisest and most experienced hunters in the Sioux tribe can be chiefs. To wear buffalo horns is a great honour. They show that the wearer has the strength and courage of a buffalo.

It will take Chased-by-Bears many years to win the 32 golden-eagle feathers he needs for a war-bonnet.

A chief can call on the spirit of the buffalo to help him when he has to make decisions.

In my grandmother's day, my people only had dogs to carry their things from camp to camp, but now we have horses. When we move, we pack everything into travel bags called parfleches. They're made from buffalo hides which we fold to keep things safe inside.

My travel bag holds my spare leggings and moccasins.

Let's make a parfleche

Find watercolour paper, 75cm x 55cm, scissors, cold tea, paints, paintbrush, string.

1 Cut the paper into the shape above. Make 24 holes around the edge. To make the paper look like hide, brush both sides with cold tea, scrunch it up, flatten it out, then let it dry.

2 Now paint a design on your parfleche and leave it to dry.

3 Fold the long sides of the parfleche inwards. Thread strings through facing holes as shown.

4 Fold the short sides inwards and lace them up, too. If you want to store something, place it in the centre of the parfleche before you fold and lace it up.

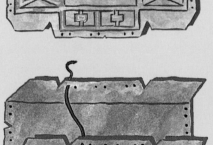

Chased-by-Bears helped father to build a bull boat like this one.

Crossing rivers

When we arrive at wide, fast-flowing rivers, Father builds a boat to get us and our things across. First, he makes a light frame, then he covers it with tough buffalo-hide. These boats are called bull boats and they move very quickly in the water. When we get to the other side, we take them apart.

Travelling by horse

When we have crossed the river, we pack up the hides and all our other goods into the parfleches. Then we load them on to a travois, which is a sort of carriage. A travois is just two long poles with a small platform in between. Sometimes it has a roof. We hitch the poles to the horse, and he pulls everything along.

When I was little, I used to sit in the back of the travois — it was very bumpy! But by the time I was five, I could ride a horse by myself and carry my own parfleche.

When we move, a horse pulls a travois along, with all our things packed inside.

You may think that life on the Plains sounds like hard work, but we do have time for fun. During the day my friends and I play games around our village. Then, in the evening we listen to stories about what life was like many years ago. Or someone plays music, and we all listen.

When the whole Sioux tribe meets up in the summer, we play lots of games.

War's Little Brother

One of my favourite games is War's Little Brother. There are up to 100 people in each team! Each player tries to hurl a ball into a huge goal. The first team to reach 12 goals wins. There aren't any rules, so it can be a bit rough. Sometimes it's just like a mini-war!

Inside the tipi, we play games marked out on buffalo hides or blankets.

Then and now...

War's Little Brother is still played in some places today, only it's called lacrosse. The teams are much smaller and there are rules which make the game safer to play.

Let's make a Sun-dance drum

Find thick card 100cm x 5cm, circle of calico 38cm in diameter, red felt 100cm x 7cm, tape, cold tea, PVA glue, paintbrush, acrylic paints, paper, stick, scissors, ribbons.

1 Bend the strip of card around and tape it. To make the fabric look like hide, brush it with cold tea, scrunch it up and let it dry.

2 Glue around the edge of the card ring. Pull the fabric tightly over the card. Hold until the glue dries. Paint a design on the drum.

3 Paint some paper triangles. Glue them on to the felt strip. Then glue the strip around the drum.

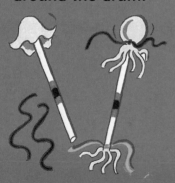

4 Wrap scraps of fabric around the end of the stick. Paint the drumstick and decorate it with ribbons.

Music of the spirits

All Sioux Indians have special songs and dances for important times, such as weddings, births and making peace. We believe that when we sing and play, spirits that live in trees, mountains, animals and rivers, can hear us.

Music isn't always for serious occasions. Eagle Dog gave Chased-by-Bears a flute for his birthday, so that he can court the girls by playing love songs!

Flutes carved from soft wood make a very sweet sound when they're played.

A special sound

The drum is an important instrument to the Sioux. Whenever we gather for the Sun-dance festival, it is always played. A holy man bangs it gently so that it sounds almost like a heartbeat.

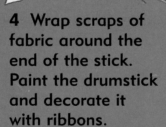

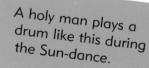
A holy man plays a drum like this during the Sun-dance.

Signs and symbols

Each Plains Indian tribe speaks its own language. Even within one tribe there are different languages. But we do have clever ways of speaking to each other and telling stories about the past.

Talking in signs

It's important for us to 'talk' to other tribes because we might need to trade, or make peace. All Indians can talk to each other using hand signals. I want to be able to trade, that's why I'm learning sign language.

I am making the sign for 'trade'. This Crow girl says that she wants to swap her beads.

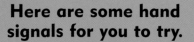

Here are some hand signals for you to try.

friend

Indian

Sioux

Crow

To make the sign for the Sioux or Crow Indians, first make the sign for Indian, followed by the sign for that tribe.

Picture stories

When we want to remember important events, we paint pictures on a buffalo hide. We call these hides 'tribal chronicles'. To read one, start in the middle and follow the pictures outwards.

This one says, "Two Indian brothers, who were buffalo hunters, walked for four days. They roped two fast horses. Then they travelled over mountains and through a forest, crossed a river and camped for the night near some hills. They heard buffalo and chased after them. They killed some buffalo and travelled back to their camp. Then they hung the meat up to dry on racks."

This buffalo hide tells the story of what happened to two braves from my village.

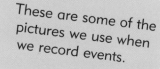

These are some of the pictures we use when we record events.

one buffalo

many buffalo

two days   Indian

Storytelling

We don't use writing, so we have to remember legends, or stories about the past. Mother says that's why we have such good memories! In our village there's a storyteller who tells us funny tales about heroes and spirits. Father says we should listen carefully to these stories because there's always a lesson to be learned from them.

All Indians believe that the world is full of spirits. The most important spirit is Wakan-Tanka, or Great Spirit. The sun is a symbol of this spirit, which is why we have a ceremony called the Sun-dance.

> When I dance and shake this rattle, I send messages to the spirits.

Animal spirits

We believe that animals have special powers that they can pass on to us. Eagle Dog has a whistle made from an eagle bone. He says it brings him good medicine.

Let's make a whistle

✴ Adult help needed

Find a piece of bamboo 12cm long, craft knife, Plasticine, string, ribbons, red feather.

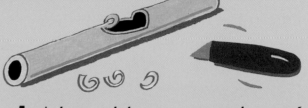

1 Ask an adult to cut a notch out of the bamboo, 5cm from one end, with the craft knife.

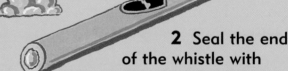

2 Seal the end of the whistle with Plasticine. Push a bit of Plasticine into the hole to block the tube. Leave a tiny gap (about 2mm) for air to pass through. Adjust the gap until you make a good sound when you blow the whistle.

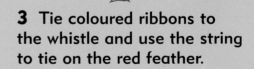

3 Tie coloured ribbons to the whistle and use the string to tie on the red feather.

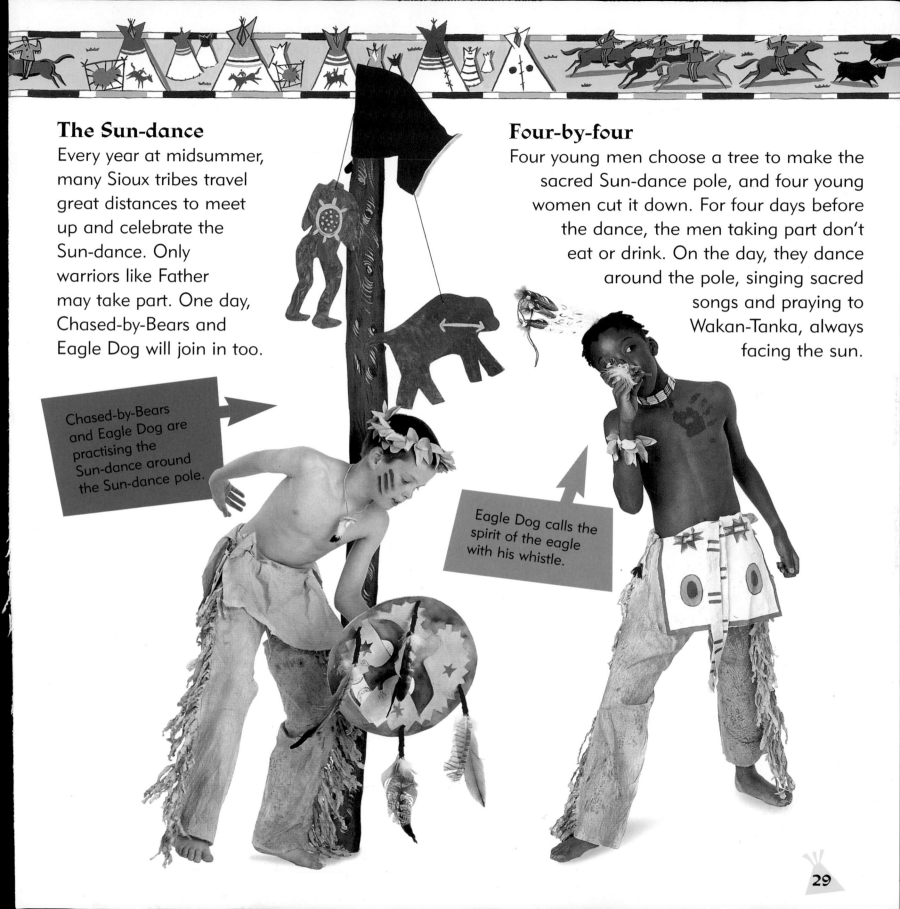

The Sun-dance

Every year at midsummer, many Sioux tribes travel great distances to meet up and celebrate the Sun-dance. Only warriors like Father may take part. One day, Chased-by-Bears and Eagle Dog will join in too.

Chased-by-Bears and Eagle Dog are practising the Sun-dance around the Sun-dance pole.

Eagle Dog calls the spirit of the eagle with his whistle.

Four-by-four

Four young men choose a tree to make the sacred Sun-dance pole, and four young women cut it down. For four days before the dance, the men taking part don't eat or drink. On the day, they dance around the pole, singing sacred songs and praying to Wakan-Tanka, always facing the sun.

29

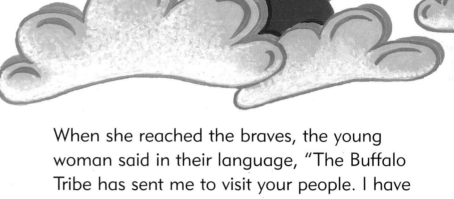

At night time, when Chased-by-Bears and I are tucked up in the tipi, Father tells us a good story. He knows this is one of my favourites because it's about a Sioux girl called White Buffalo.

A beautiful young woman

One autumn, many years ago, two Sioux braves rode out across the Plains in search of buffalo. The people of their village were very hungry and if they did not eat soon, they would starve.

After roaming the Plains for a few days, with no luck, the braves suddenly saw a beautiful young woman coming towards them. She wore a fringed dress, leggings and moccasins. Her hair was tied with a tuft of white-buffalo hide and her face was painted with stripes. In her hand she carried a fan made from the leaves of a special healing plant, called sage.

When she reached the braves, the young woman said in their language, "The Buffalo Tribe has sent me to visit your people. I have something important to give you which will help you in the future. Go home and tell your chief to build a special tipi. There must be a seat of honour covered with sage, and a buffalo skull behind it. I will arrive at sunrise tomorrow."

The mysterious guest

The braves raced home and told the rest of the village what had happened. Everyone immediately set to work, building a special tipi, as the young woman had instructed them.

The next morning, just before daybreak, everyone gathered to wait for the guest. As the sun rose, they saw the young woman walking towards the village. She was dressed exactly as before, but this time, she carried a pipe.

A precious gift

The chief led the beautiful woman into the tipi and showed her the seat of honour. Then he said, "Today the Great Spirit, Wakan-Tanka, has smiled on us by sending this maiden to rescue us in our time of need. We have great respect for our guest, but we are poor people and only have water to offer you."

As he spoke, the chief dipped a blade of sweetgrass into a buffalo horn filled with water. The woman took it and said, "Brothers and sisters, you are good people. The Buffalo Tribe has sent me to give you this pipe. If you need buffalo to eat, smoke it and they will be sent. This pipe must only be used for good – smoke it and it will cure the sick and help you make peace with your enemies. Remember, everything you need in life comes from the Earth, the Sun and the Winds. Always show them respect."

The white buffalo calf

Then she lit the pipe and offered it first to Wakan-Tanka, then to the Earth, the four Winds and the Sun before passing it to the chief. "I have done my work and now I must return to the Buffalo Tribe," she said. The people of the village parted to let the woman pass. But as she turned to leave, the young woman suddenly changed into a beautiful, white buffalo calf, one of the rarest creatures of all. From that day on, the pipe was always called the White Buffalo Calf Pipe and it is still one of the most precious objects to the Sioux tribe.

The world of White Buffalo

White Buffalo and her friends lived over a hundred years ago. Today we know about her world because there are many Plains Indians living in North America who still practise the old Sioux customs and way of life.

Where the Sioux live

Nowadays, many Sioux live, work and study in cities in North America. But some still live in tipis and other homes on the Plains, on huge areas of land called reservations.

Plains Indians today

No matter where they live, Plains Indians are proud of their ways and beliefs. Some Sioux still celebrate the Sun-dance festival, and make clothes and moccasins in the old way. The art of storytelling is alive too. Parents tell their children stories about their ancestors and the spirits that rule the Indian world, so that the old ways will not be forgotten.

Tribal chronicles tell us about important events in the history of the Plains Indians.

Index

The words in **bold** are things that you can make.